IT'S FUN TO LEARN ABOUT
SUMS

Claire Llewellyn
Consultant: Dr Naima Browne

ARMADILLO

NOTES

$8-1=7$

$6+0=6$

$2 \times 10 = 20$

$4 \times 2 = 8$

$6 \div 2 = 3$

This book introduces children to the concepts of addition, subtraction, multiplication and division. It is designed for children who already understand the concepts of matching, sorting and classifying and who can recognize and understand the number symbols 1 to 50. It will provide your child with a sound basis for the arithmetic covered in the first years of school.

Reading together

The mathematical word 'sum' means 'total'. We have chosen to apply the word 'sum' to all equations because it is easily recognized. You can help your child by reading aloud the words that accompany the pictures. Go through the book at the child's own pace. Doing sums can be tiring. Maybe look at just one topic at a time, and allow a few days for the ideas to sink in. Always make reading times enjoyable.

Talking it through

Do not worry if your child has trouble in finding the correct answers. Making mistakes is a valuable part of learning. It is much more important for children to explain their answers and to be cheerful and confident. By exploring the world of numbers together, and providing a supportive atmosphere, you will be helping your child to enjoy their first taste of mathematics.

Learning by doing

Encourage your child to try the activities. They can help to extend and develop skills. Check your child's understanding by using sums in your daily life – tidying the cupboards or going to the shops provide plenty of opportunities for sums. Always remember to praise children when they answer correctly.

The number line

Some pages in the book have number lines to help children to add up and take away. Number lines are fun and easy to use. To do the sum $3 + 2$, put your finger on number 3 in the line and count forward 2 more places. This gives you the answer. To do the sum $5 - 3$, put your finger on number 5 in the line and count back 3 places to find the answer.

0   1   2   3   4   5

CONTENTS

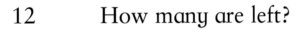
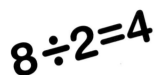

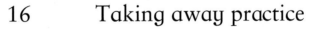
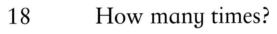

$8 \div 2 = 4$

$6 \div 2 = 3$

$3 + 5 = 8$

$5 \times 3 = 15$

Are there enough?

Four toys are going to the seaside. They are taking all these different things. Do they have enough, too many or too few?

Are there enough sandwiches for all the toys?

Does each toy have a bag?

Do the toys all have surfboards to ride the waves?

Can you count the swimming goggles?

Four cuddly toys are going to the seaside.

How many rubber rings are there?

Count the towels. Are there enough?

Are there the same number of inflatable rafts as there are toys?

The toys like swimming. Do they have enough snorkels?

Is there a swimming cap for everyone?

4

Six aliens are having a day out in space.
Can you count all the things they see?

Count the pretty planets. Is there one for every alien?

How many stars are twinkling in the sky?

Each alien needs its own spaceship. Are there enough?

Six friendly aliens from outer space.

How many heavy suitcases are there? Each alien needs just one.

Space travel makes you thirsty. Will everyone have a delicious drink?

Every alien needs a robot. Are there too many here?

Yum, yum! It's teatime! But are there enough cakes to go around?

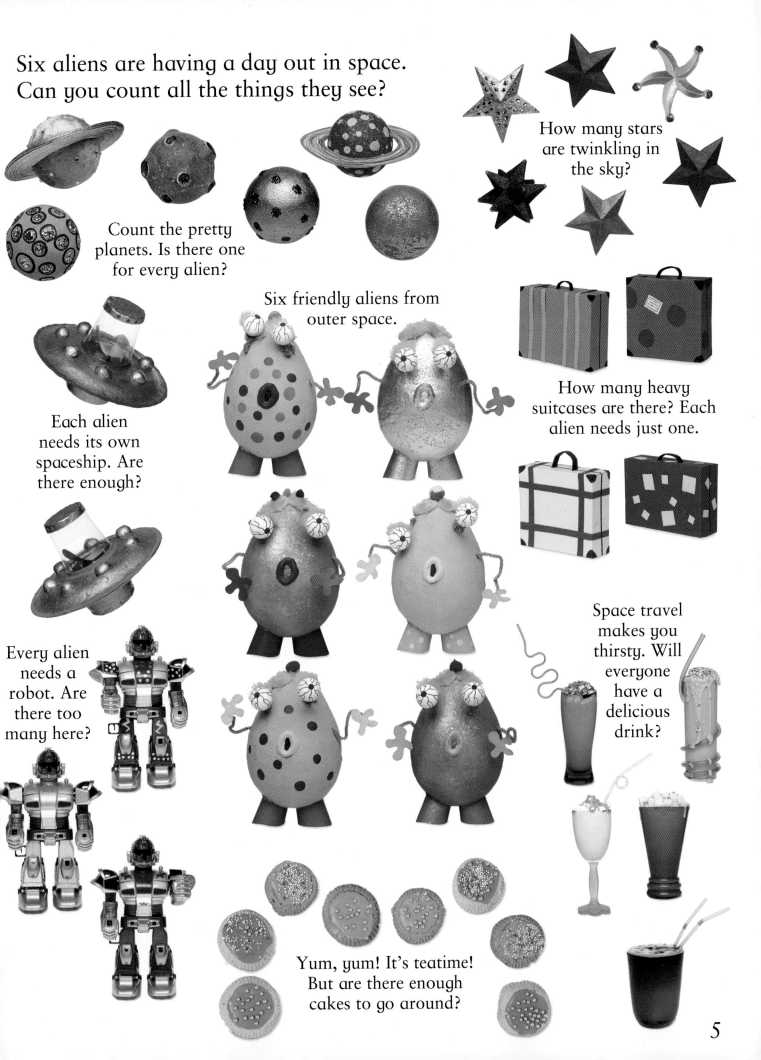

How many altogether?

When you add two things together you can make a sum. In a sum, you use numbers and signs instead of words.

This sign means add together.

This sign means equals.

This is how you write the sum.

1+2=3

1 teddy acrobat

2 more teddy acrobats

3 teddy acrobats altogether

This is how you write the sum.

2+0=2

2 circus clowns

0 clowns

2 circus clowns altogether

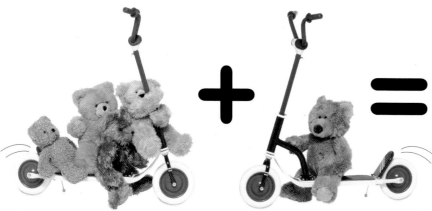

This is how you write the sum.

4+1=5

4 teddies on a scooter

1 more teddy on a scooter

5 teddies altogether

This is how you write the sum.

2+2=4

2 creepy-crawlies on the trapeze

2 more creepy-crawlies

4 creepy-crawlies altogether

Did you know?

A calculator helps people to do sums. It has a small keyboard and a display screen. There is a key for each number from 0 to 9, and keys for doing different types of sum, such as +. You press the key for each figure and type the sum you want to do. Press = and then the answer comes up on the screen.

This is how you write the sum.

1+3=4

1 juggler

3 more jugglers

4 jugglers altogether

Use this number line to help you add up. It goes from 0 to 5.

0   1   2   3   4

Adding up

This page is full of children and toys enjoying a party with their friends. Can you do all the adding up sums?

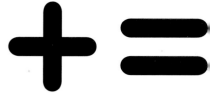

This sign means add together.

This sign means equals.

 +  =

This is how you write the sum.

5+2=7

5 presents

2 more presents

7 presents altogether

 =

This is how you write the sum.

6+0=6

6 dancing toys

0 toys

6 dancing toys altogether

Try this!

Draw the sum shown below on a piece of paper. How many clowns and jugglers are there altogether?

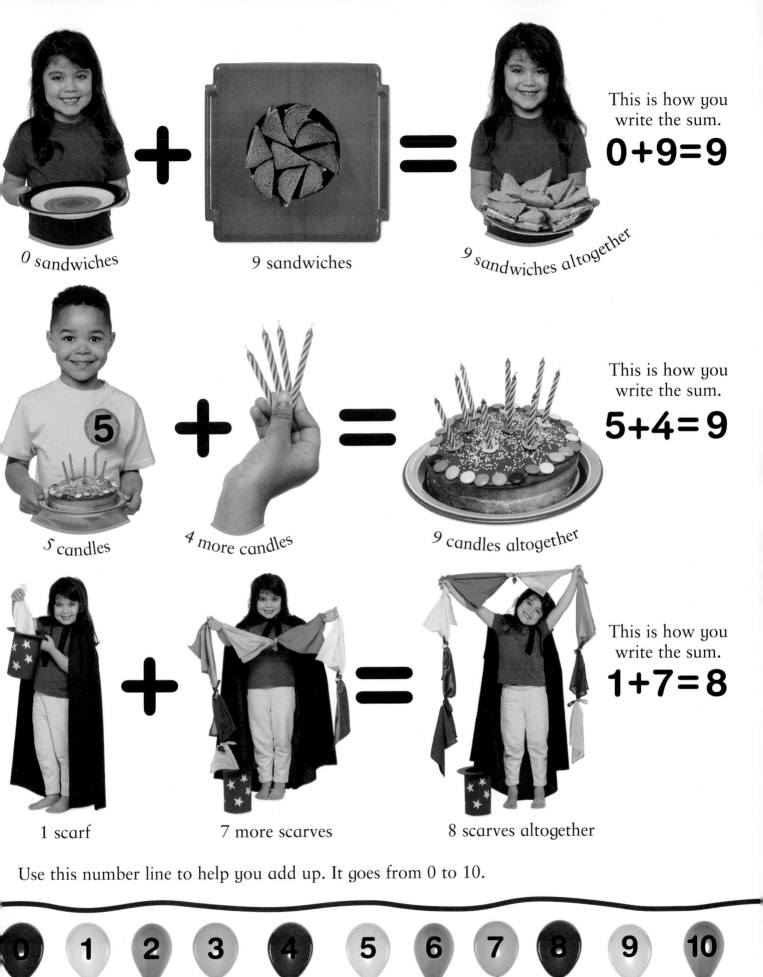

0 sandwiches + 9 sandwiches = 9 sandwiches altogether

This is how you write the sum.

0+9=9

5 candles + 4 more candles = 9 candles altogether

This is how you write the sum.

5+4=9

1 scarf + 7 more scarves = 8 scarves altogether

This is how you write the sum.

1+7=8

Use this number line to help you add up. It goes from 0 to 10.

0 1 2 3 4 5 6 7 8 9 10

Adding up practice

These creepy-crawlies are busy working, eating, crawling and flying. How many are there in each sum?

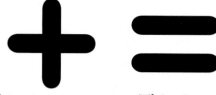

This sign means add together.

This sign means equals

8 hungry flies

10 more flies

How many flies altogether?

This is how you write the sum.

8+10=?

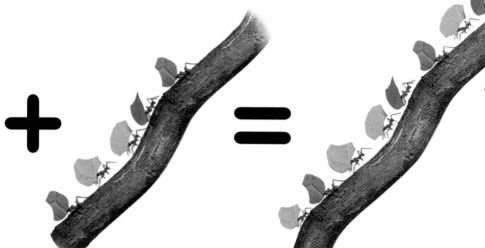

3 busy ants

5 more ants

How many ants altogether?

This is how you write the sum.

3+5=?

14 buzzy bees

6 more bees

How many bees altogether?

This is how you write the sum.

14+6=?

Use this number line to help you add up. It goes all the way from 0 to 20.

0 1 2 3 4 5 6 7 8 9 10

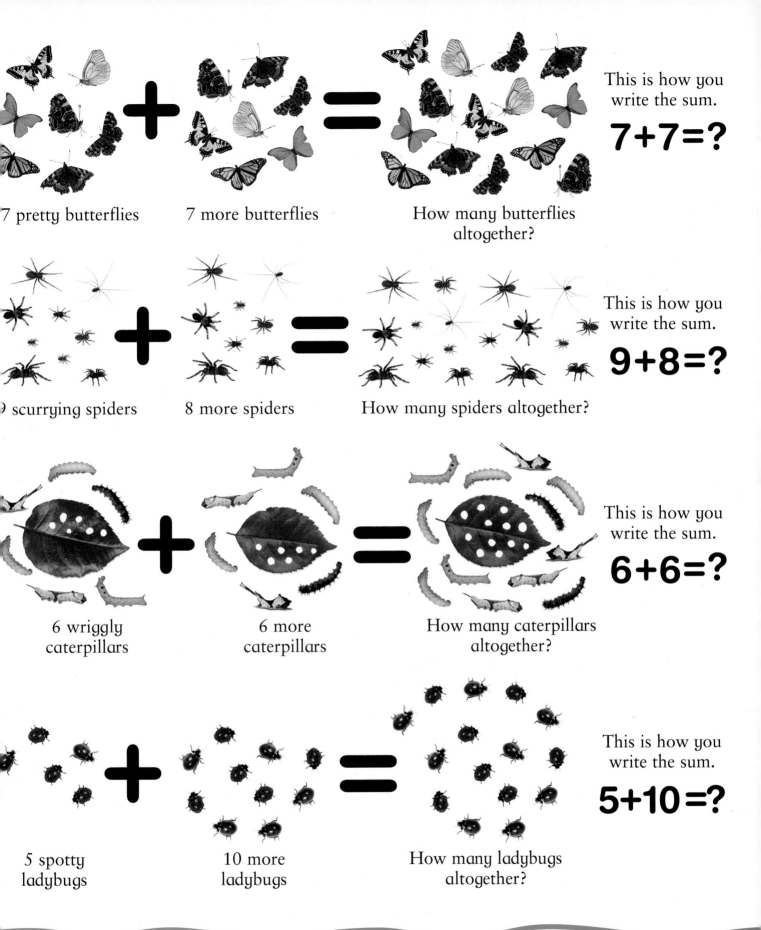

7 pretty butterflies   7 more butterflies

How many butterflies altogether?

This is how you write the sum.

7+7=?

9 scurrying spiders   8 more spiders

How many spiders altogether?

This is how you write the sum.

9+8=?

6 wriggly caterpillars   6 more caterpillars

How many caterpillars altogether?

This is how you write the sum.

6+6=?

5 spotty ladybugs   10 more ladybugs

How many ladybugs altogether?

This is how you write the sum.

5+10=?

11   12   13   14   15   16   17   18   19   20

How many are left?

To work out the difference between two sets of numbers, we take one away from the other. This is another sort of sum, and it is called taking away.

– This sign means take away.

= This sign means equals.

5 ice creams — The teds take 2 away = 3 ice creams are left

This is how you write the sum.

5–2=3

2 rubber rings — Swimmers take 2 away = 0 rubber rings are left

This is how you write the sum.

2–2=0

5 books in a pile — The teds take 1 to read = 4 books are left

This is how you write the sum.

5–1=4

 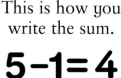   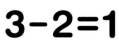 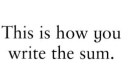

3 teds on a scooter — 2 teds fall off = 1 ted is left

This is how you write the sum.

3–2=1

12

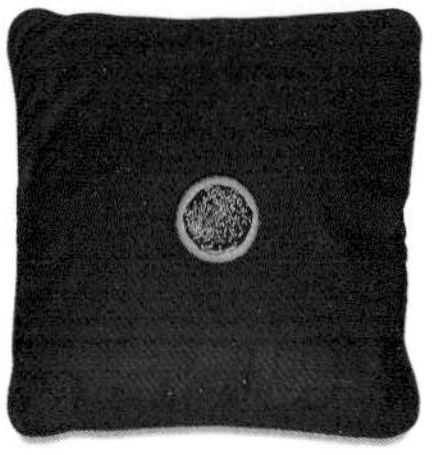

1 cookie on
a pillow

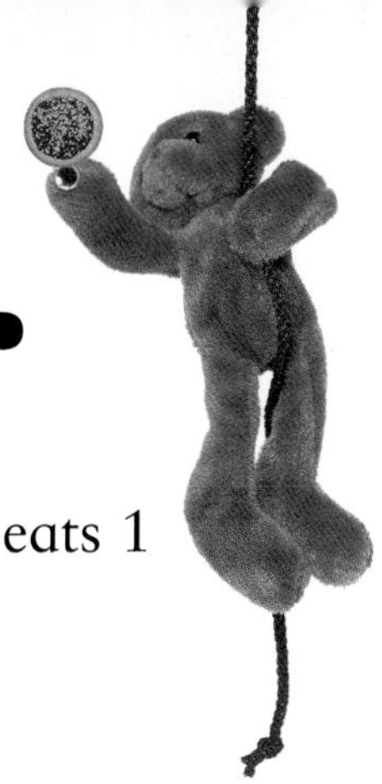

Ted eats 1

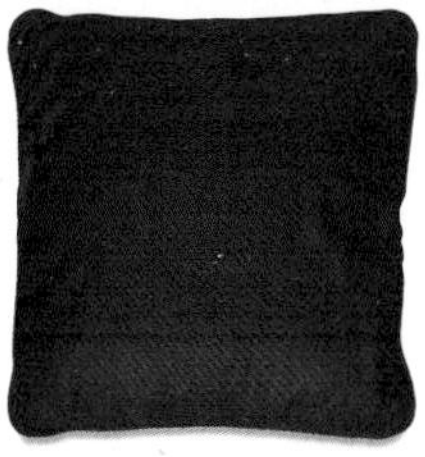

0 cookies are left

This is how you
write the sum.

1-1=0

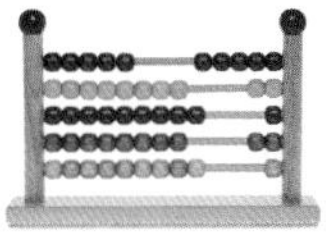

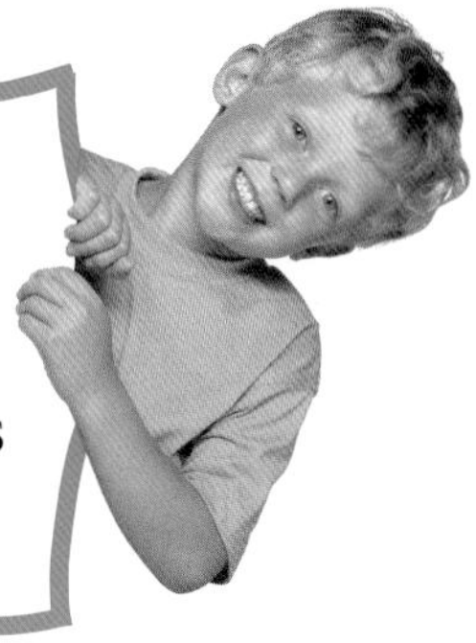

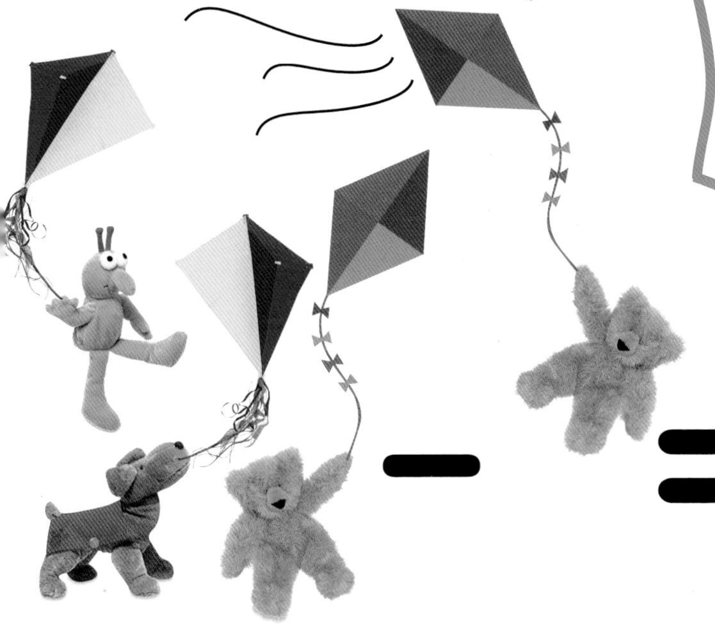

3 toys are flying kites

1 toy floats off

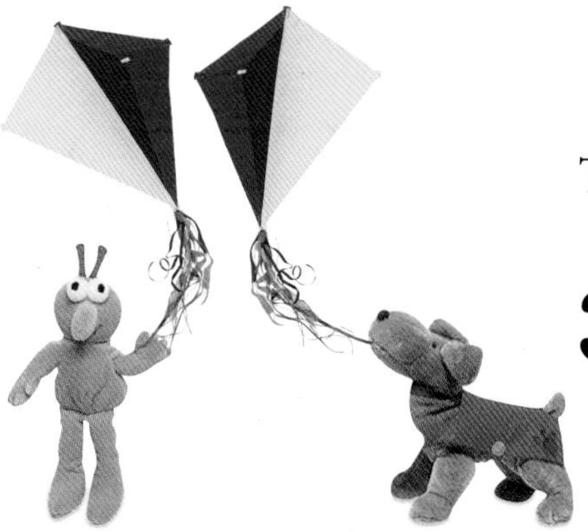

2 toys are left

This is how you
write the sum.

3-1=2

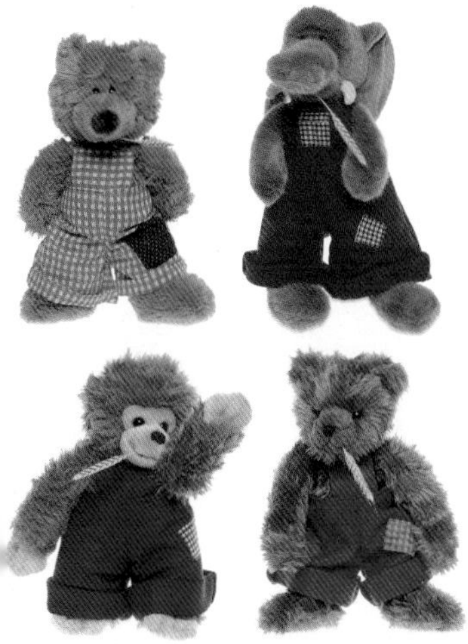

4 farmers at work

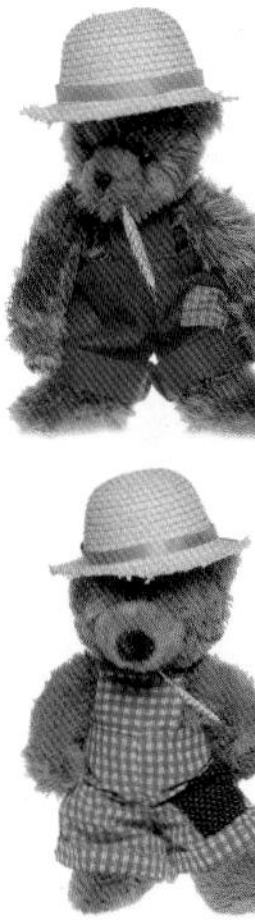

2 farmers go home

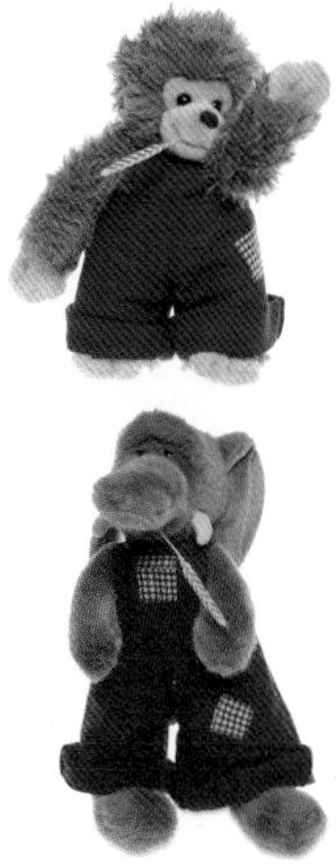

2 farmers are left

This is how you
write the sum.

4-2=2

Use this number line to help you take away. It goes from 0 to 5.

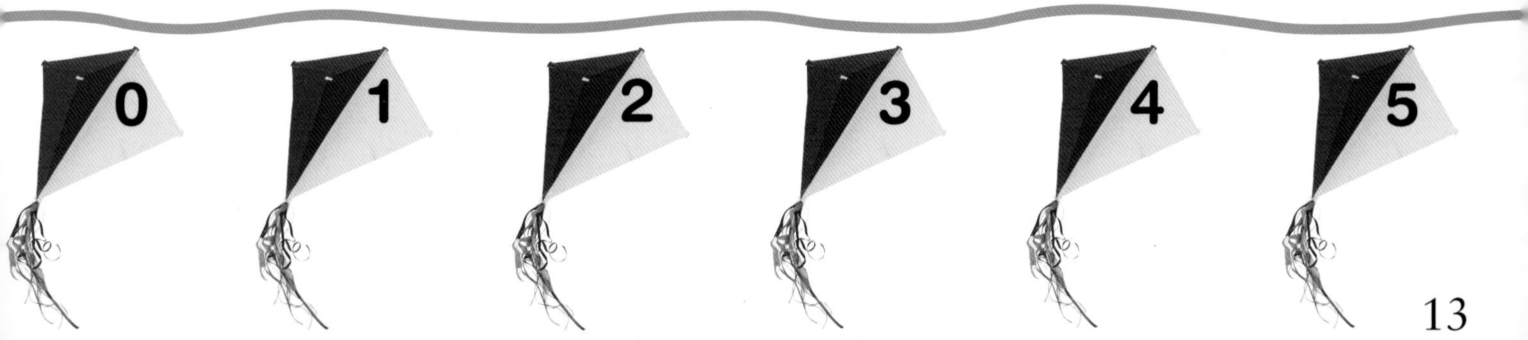

0   1   2   3   4   5

Taking away

There are lots of hungry animals on this page. Work out how much food they have eaten and how much food is left.

This sign means take away.

This sign means equals.

8 bananas hanging on a tree

Monkey takes 1

7 bananas are left

This is how you write the sum.

8-1=7

10 sweet apples

Tortoise eats 5

5 apples are left

This is how you write the sum.

10-5=5

7 chunks of tasty cheese

Mouse eats 5

2 chunks are left

This is how you write the sum.

7-5=2

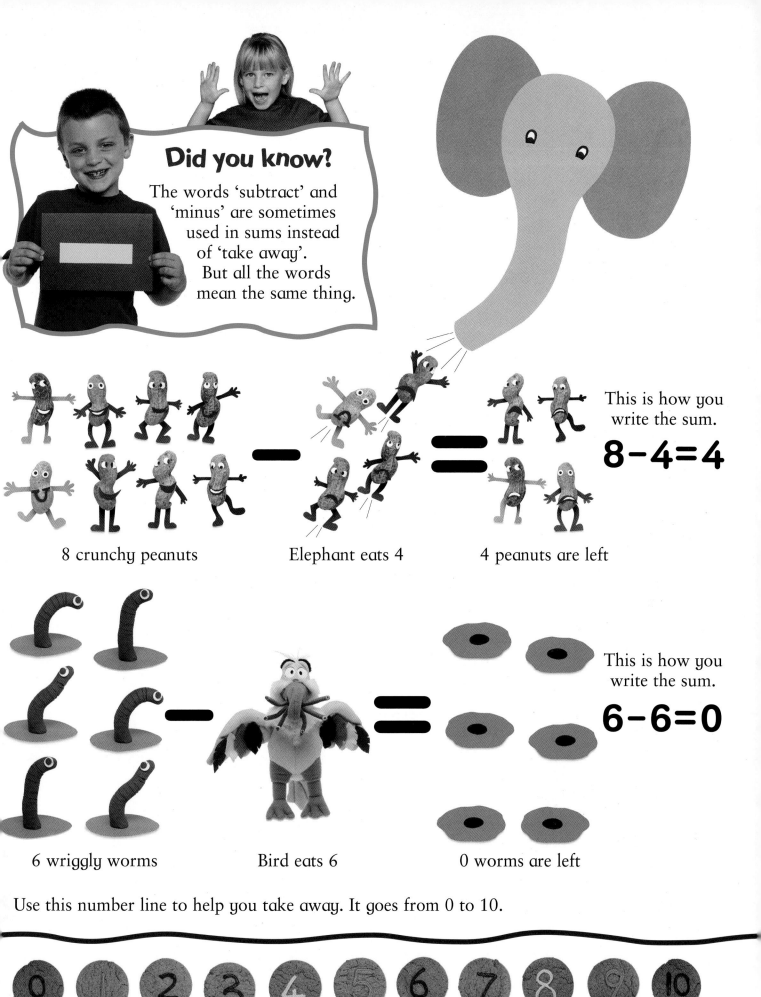

Did you know?

The words 'subtract' and 'minus' are sometimes used in sums instead of 'take away'. But all the words mean the same thing.

This is how you write the sum.

8-4=4

8 crunchy peanuts   Elephant eats 4   4 peanuts are left

This is how you write the sum.

6-6=0

6 wriggly worms   Bird eats 6   0 worms are left

Use this number line to help you take away. It goes from 0 to 10.

0   1   2   3   4   5   6   7   8   9   10

Taking away practice

Here is a chance for you to try some more take away sums. Can you work out the answers to these?

This sign means take away. This sign means equal

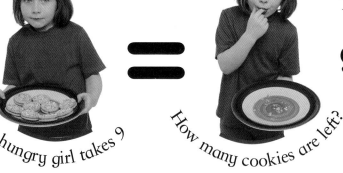

This is how you write the sum.

9-9=?

9 cookies on a plate — A hungry girl takes 9 — How many cookies are left?

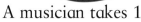

This is how you write the sum.

6-1=?

6 musical instruments — A musician takes 1 — How many instruments are left?

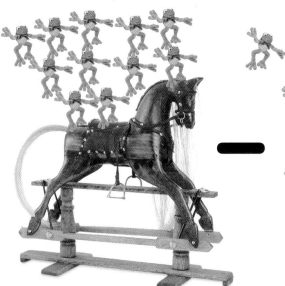

This is how you write the sum.

11-4=?

11 frogs balancing — 4 frogs fall off — How many frogs are left?

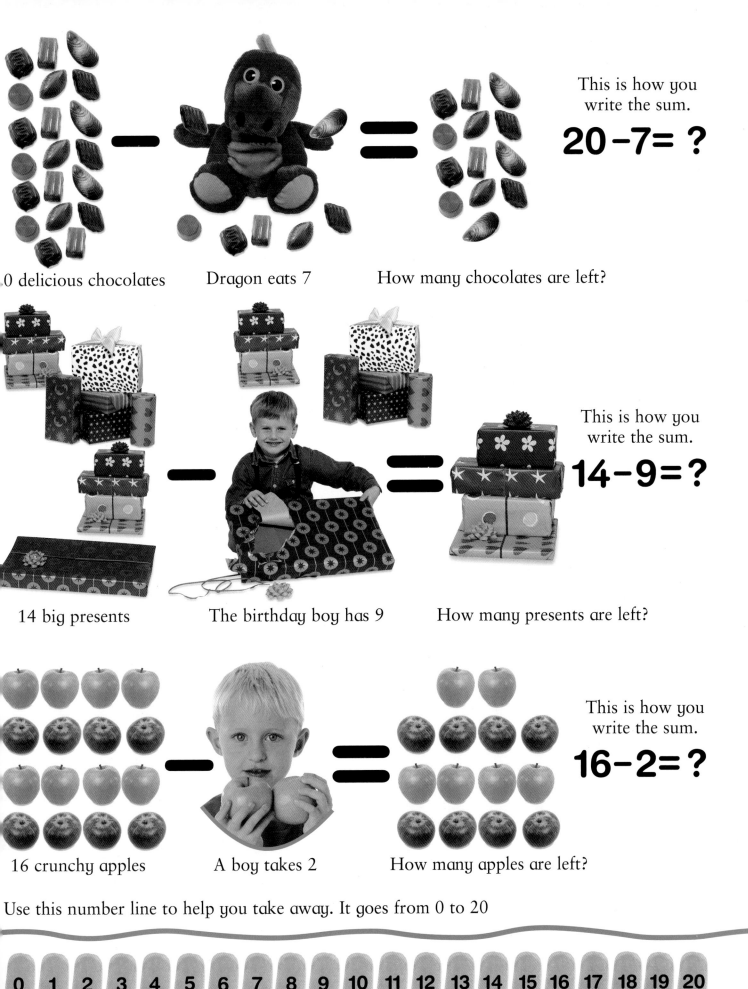

20 delicious chocolates   Dragon eats 7   How many chocolates are left?

This is how you write the sum.

20 - 7 = ?

14 big presents   The birthday boy has 9   How many presents are left?

This is how you write the sum.

14 - 9 = ?

16 crunchy apples   A boy takes 2   How many apples are left?

This is how you write the sum.

16 - 2 = ?

Use this number line to help you take away. It goes from 0 to 20

0 1 2 3 4 5 6 7 8 9 10 11 12 13 14 15 16 17 18 19 20

How many times?

Sometimes you have to count groups of things.
Multiplying is quick way of counting them.
For this kind of sum we use the times sign.

This sign means times.

This sign means equal

This is how you write the sum.

2x2=4

There are 2 children

Each child has 2 legs

There are 4 legs altogether

This is how you write the sum.

3x2=6

There are 3 children

Each child has 2 arms

There are 6 arms altogether

This is how you write the sum.

5x3=15

Each hat has 5 bobbles

There are 3 hats

There are 15 bobbles altogether

18

Try this!

Find a few pairs of gloves and socks, and lay them on the floor. How many gloves and socks are there altogether? Try making some more sums using the x sign.

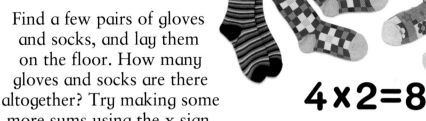

4×2=8

   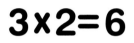

3×2=6

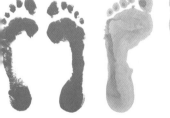 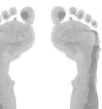 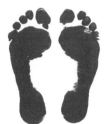  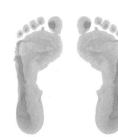

This is how you write the sum.

4×2=8

There are 4 pairs of socks   Each pair has 2 socks   There are 8 socks altogether

This is how you write the sum.

5×2=10

There are 5 pairs of feet   Each pair has 2 feet   There are 10 feet altogether

  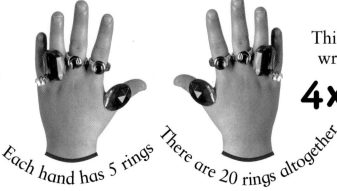

This is how you write the sum.

4×5=20

How many rings?   There are 4 hands   Each hand has 5 rings   There are 20 rings altogether

19

More times

All the things on this page are arranged in groups. Try doing the times sums to find out how many things there are altogether.

This sign means times. This sign means equal

There are 2 lines of fish

There are 4 fish in each line

This is how you write the sum.

2×4=8

There are 3 groups of starfish   There are 10 starfish in each group

This is how you write the sum.

3×10=30

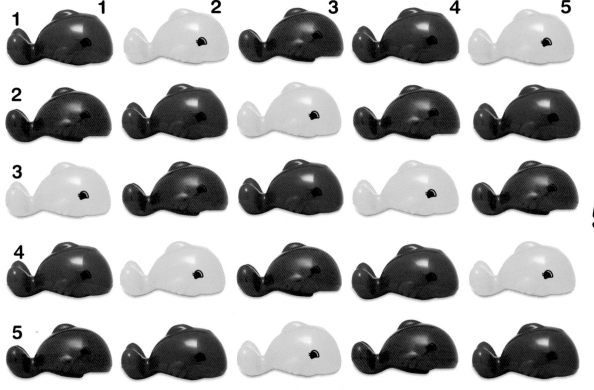

There are 5 rows of whales   There are 5 whales in each row

This is how you write the sum.

5×5=25

20

There are 2 groups of shells   There are 8 shells in each group

This is how you write the sum.

2×8=16

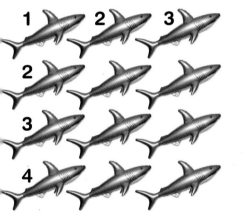 

There are 5 groups of lobsters   There are 6 lobsters in each group

This is how you write the sum.

5×6=30

There are 2 groups of sharks   There are 12 sharks in each group

This is how you write the sum.

2×12=24

There are 5 rows of crabs   There are 10 crabs in each row

This is how you write the sum.

5×10=50

Times tables

You'll soon start to learn your times tables. Knowing them off by heart helps you to do sums *F-A-S-T*.

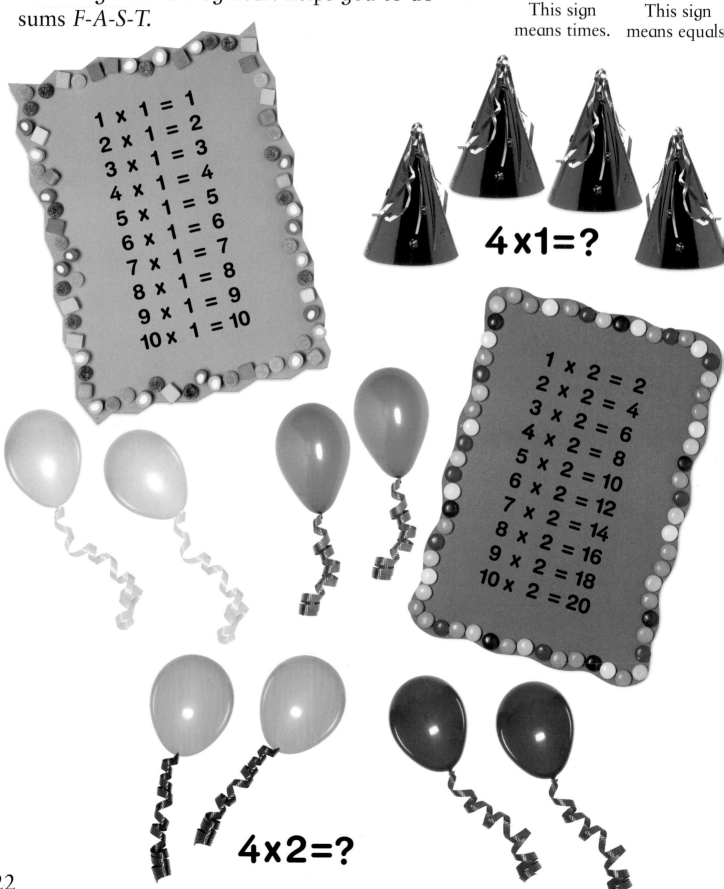

$$1 \times 1 = 1$$
$$2 \times 1 = 2$$
$$3 \times 1 = 3$$
$$4 \times 1 = 4$$
$$5 \times 1 = 5$$
$$6 \times 1 = 6$$
$$7 \times 1 = 7$$
$$8 \times 1 = 8$$
$$9 \times 1 = 9$$
$$10 \times 1 = 10$$

$$4 \times 1 = ?$$

$$1 \times 2 = 2$$
$$2 \times 2 = 4$$
$$3 \times 2 = 6$$
$$4 \times 2 = 8$$
$$5 \times 2 = 10$$
$$6 \times 2 = 12$$
$$7 \times 2 = 14$$
$$8 \times 2 = 16$$
$$9 \times 2 = 18$$
$$10 \times 2 = 20$$

$$4 \times 2 = ?$$

$1 \times 5 = 5$
$2 \times 5 = 10$
$3 \times 5 = 15$
$4 \times 5 = 20$
$5 \times 5 = 25$
$6 \times 5 = 30$
$7 \times 5 = 35$
$8 \times 5 = 40$
$9 \times 5 = 45$
$10 \times 5 = 50$

$2 \times 3 = ?$

Try this!

Learn your times tables

It's a good idea to learn your times tables by heart. To make learning fun, try reciting a times table while you hop or skip on the spot. Work through the table, saying each sum out loud. Try to keep in time with each hop!

$1 \times 10 = 10$
$2 \times 10 = 20$
$3 \times 10 = 30$
$4 \times 10 = 40$
$5 \times 10 = 50$
$6 \times 10 = 60$
$7 \times 10 = 70$
$8 \times 10 = 80$
$9 \times 10 = 90$
$10 \times 10 = 100$

$2 \times 10 = ?$

Share it out

Two wicked pirate chiefs are sharing out the treasure. How much should each one have?

Pirate Pete

How many hats will Pete and Penny get?

4 maps of buried treasure

How many different jewels are there? How many will each pirate have?

Share out the flags between the pirate chiefs.

caw-caw!

caw-caw!

Will each pirate get a parrot?

Is there a shovel for each pirate?

These fierce teddies are the pirate ship crew.

Is there a
tankard for
both pirates?

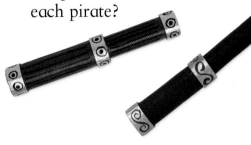

Count up the telescopes.
How many are there for
each pirate?

How will you share out
this glittering gold?

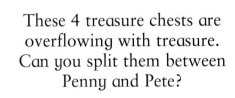

Pirate Penny

10 wooden
barrels full of
confectionery.
Can you share
it between the
two pirates?

These 4 treasure chests are
overflowing with treasure.
Can you split them between
Penny and Pete?

How many teddies does each pirate chief get?

25

Divide it up

Sometimes you need to share out lots of things. Dividing is a way of making equal groups. Another word for this is sharing.

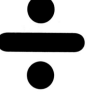

This sign means divide by.

This sign means equals.

6 pretty ribbons

2 cows

Each cow has 3 pretty ribbons

This is how you write the sum.

6÷2=3

10 lumps of sugar

2 horses

Each horse has 5 lumps of sugar

This is how you write the sum.

10÷2=5

2 eggs

2 hens

Each hen has 1 egg

This is how you write the sum.

2÷2=1

Try this!

1. Take a piece of paper and draw 2 farmers, 2 hats, 4 cows and 6 horses.
2. Cut the pictures out.
3. How many hats, cows and horses for each farmer?

Try writing this as three sums, using the ÷ sign.

This is how you write the sum.

20÷5=4

20 sheep   5 sheepdogs   Each sheepdog has 4 sheep

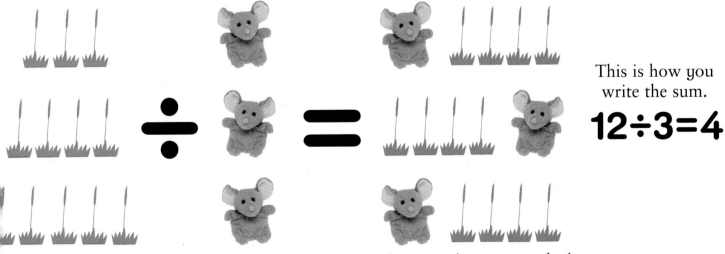

This is how you write the sum.

12÷3=4

2 ears of wheat   3 mice   Each mouse has 4 ears of wheat

27

More division

It's time to try some more division with these teddy sums. Can you work out all the answers?

This sign means divide by.

This sign means equals

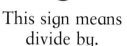

20 candies

5 hungry teds

How many candies does each ted get?

This is how you write the sum.

20÷5=?

4 buckets

2 teds

How many buckets does each ted hold?

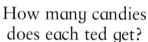

This is how you write the sum.

4÷2=?

6 magic wands   6 magician teds

How many wands does each ted get?

This is how you write the sum.

6÷6=?

28

10 delicious cakes   5 hungry teds   How many cakes does each ted get?

This is how you write the sum.

10÷5=?

2 tennis rackets   2 teds   How many rackets does each ted get?

This is how you write the sum.

2÷2=?

5 rubber ducks   5 teds   How many ducks does each ted get?

This is how you write the sum.

15÷5=?

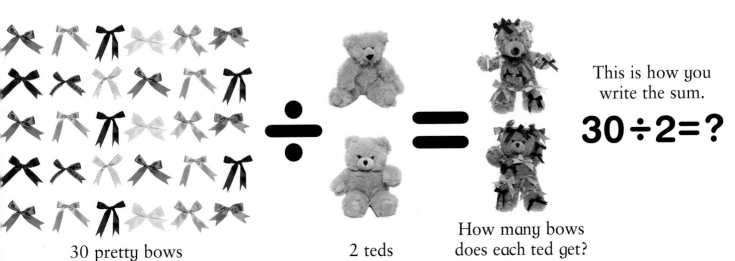

30 pretty bows   2 teds   How many bows does each ted get?

This is how you write the sum.

30÷2=?

29

The sums game

Take it in turns to roll a die and move your markers around the board. Each time you land on an 'add together' or 'times' symbol, work out the answer to the sum and go forward that number. When you land on a 'take away' or 'divide by' symbol, work out the answer to the sum and go back that number. The first person to finish wins.

You will need:

markers or buttons

die

1

2

3

4

$1+1=?$

5

6

7

11

10

$3\times2=?$

9

$10-4=?$ 8

12

13

14

15 $6\div2=?$

16

17

$1+0=?$

18

19

20 $9-6=?$

30

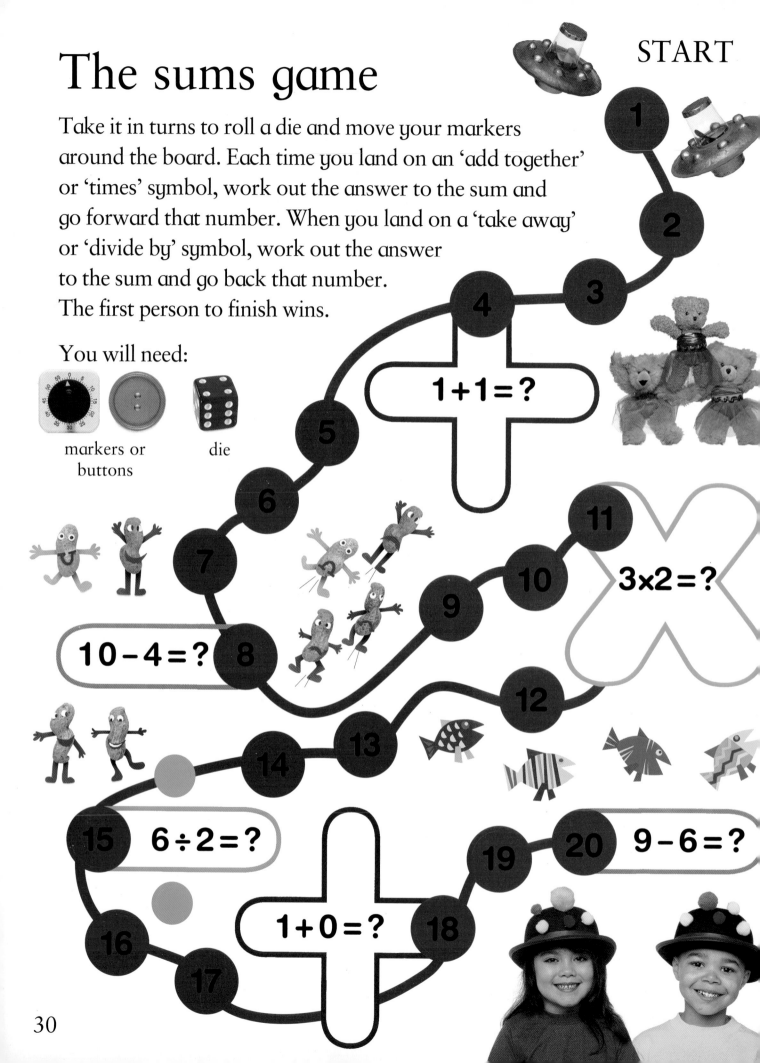

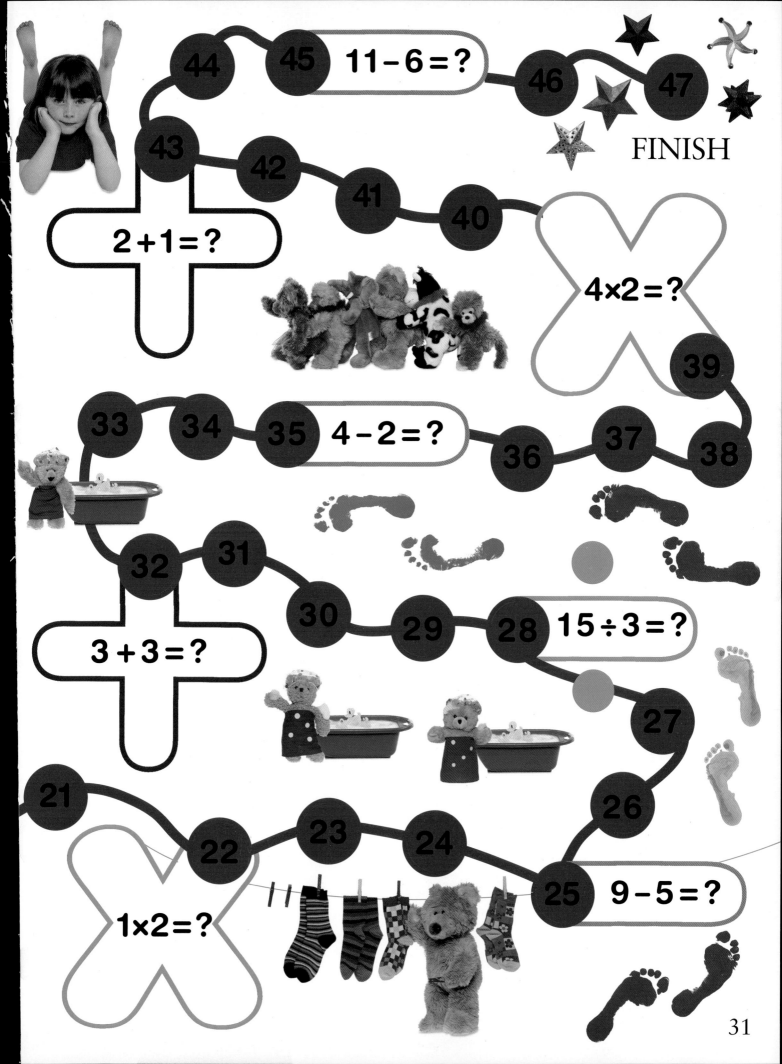

44

45

11 − 6 = ?

46

47

FINISH

43

42

41

40

2 + 1 = ?

4×2 = ?

39

33

34

35

4 − 2 = ?

36

37

38

32

31

30

29

28

15 ÷ 3 = ?

3 + 3 = ?

27

21

26

22

23

24

25

9 − 5 = ?

1×2 = ?

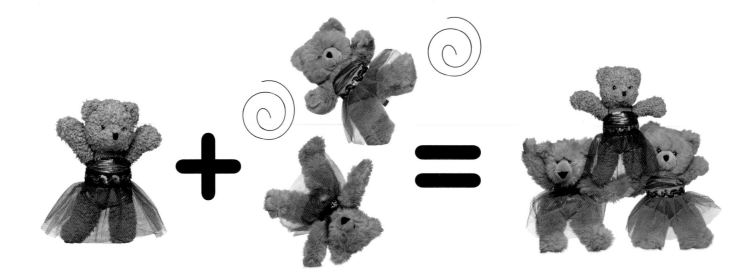

This edition is published by Armadillo,
an imprint of Anness Publishing Ltd,
108 Great Russell Street,
London WC1B 3NA;
info@anness.com

www.annesspublishing.com; twitter: @Anness_Books

Anness Publishing has a new picture agency outlet
for images for publishing, promotions or advertising.
Please visit our website www.practicalpictures.com
for more information.

© Anness Publishing Ltd 2015

A CIP catalogue record for this book
is available from the British Library.

Publisher: Joanna Lorenz
Senior Editor: Felicity Forster
Educational Consultant: Dr Naima Browne,
    Department of Education, University of London
Photography: John Freeman
Stylist: Melanie Williams
Designer: Louise Millar, Mike Leaman Design Partners
Production Controller: Ben Worley

Manufacturer: Anness Publishing Ltd,
108 Great Russell Street, London WC1B 3NA, England
For Product Tracking go to: www.annesspublishing.com/tracking
Batch: 7558-23944-1127

ACKNOWLEDGEMENTS
The publisher would like to thank the following children for
appearing in this book: Alexa, Alexander, Cimarron, Cleo,
Daisy, Daisy, Eloise, Faye, Holly, Jack, Lecia, Luke, Madison,
Matthew, Molly, Sean, Tom.

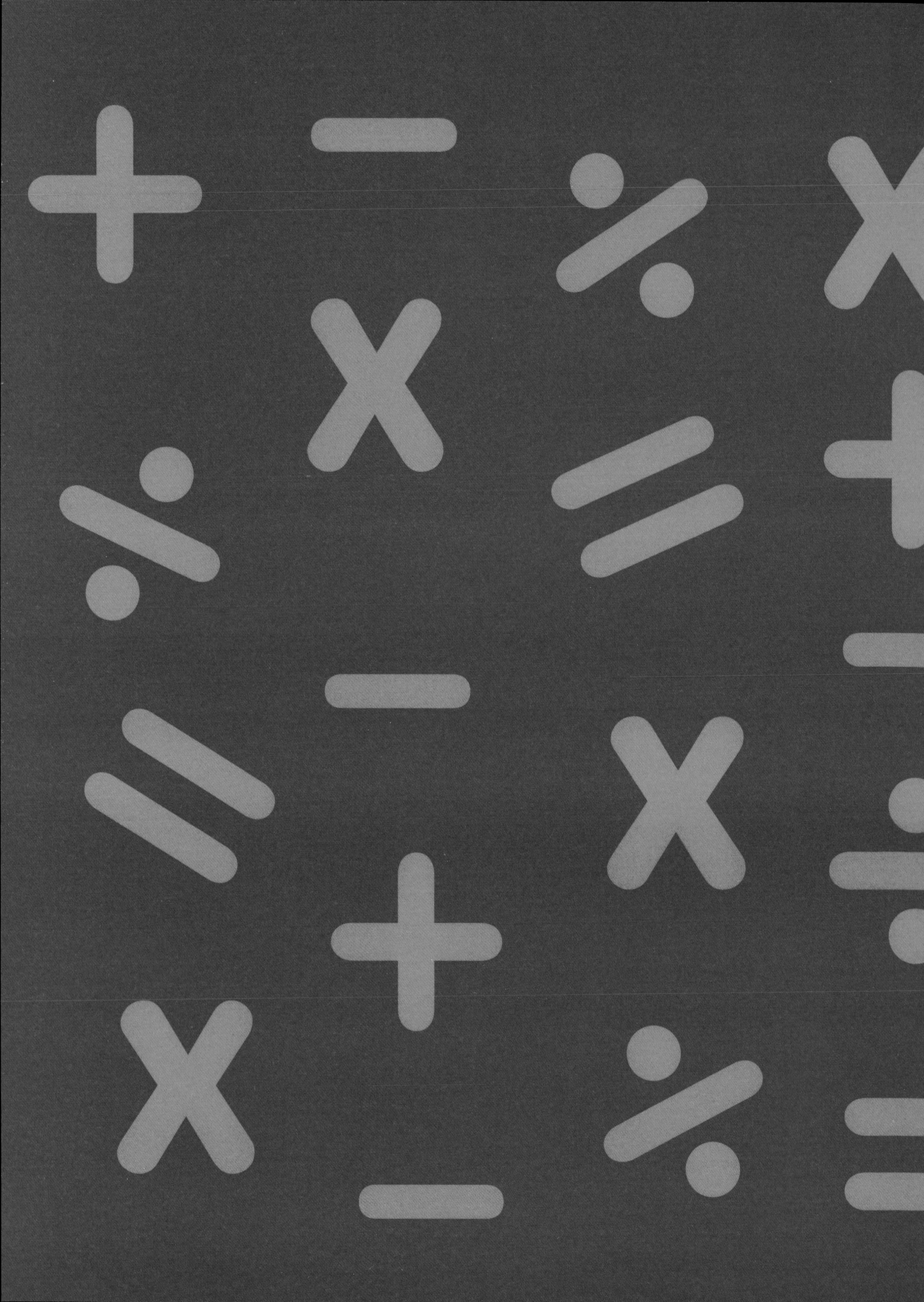